Celebrate Spring

Planting Seeds

by Kathryn Clay

raintree

a Capstone company — publishers for children

Edited by Erika L. Shores
Designed by Juliette Peters and Ashlee Suker
Picture research by Svetlana Zhurkin
Production by Katy LaVigne
Originated by Capstone Global Library
Printed and bound in China.

ISBN 978 1 4747 1238 5

19 18 17 16 15
10 9 8 7 6 5 4 3 2 1

British Library Cataloguing in Publication Data
A full catalogue record for this book is available from the British Library.

Acknowledgements
We would like to thank the following for permission to reproduce photographs: Capstone Studio: Karon Dubke, cover; Dreamstime: Branex, 15, Wally Stemberger, 7; Getty Images: Superstudio, 21; iStockphoto: MKucova, 1; Newscom: Blend Images/KidStock, 19; Shutterstock: Africa Studio, 3, caldix, 13, Filipe B. Varela, 9, Maks Narodenko, 15 (inset), Pressmaster, 17, Stockr, 5, TwilightArtPictures, 11, USBFCO, back cover and throughout.

Every effort has been made to contact copyright holders of material reproduced in this book. Any omissions will be rectified in subsequent printings if notice is given to the publisher.

Contents

Spring is here!

Cold winter weather ends.

It's time to plant seeds.

From seed to plant

Seeds need rain and sun.

Spring storms water the seeds.

Seeds crack open.

Roots push down.

Seeds push up from the soil.
They are called shoots.

Green leaves grow.

Small buds form.

Then the flowers bloom.

Who plants seeds?

A farmer plants seeds.

Plants grow tall in fields.

A gardener plants seeds.

She grows food in her garden.

Ms Silver's class plants seeds.

They grow grass.

Sam and his dad plant seeds.

They grow flowers.

What seeds will you plant?

Glossary

bloom   produce a flower

bud   part of a plant that turns into a leaf or flower

root   part of a plant that attaches to the ground

seed   tiny plant part from which a new plant grows

shoot   stem growing out of a seed that becomes the plant

Find out more

All About Seeds (All About Plants), Claire Throp (Raintree, 2014)

Harvest Festival (Holidays and Festivals), Nancy Dickmann (Raintree, 2011)

Seed to Plant (National Geographic Readers: Level 1), Kristin Baird Rattini (National Geographic Society, 2014)

Internet sites

www.bbc.co.uk/education/clips/zc62tfr
Watch a video about growing seeds.

www.education.com/worksheets/weather-seasons
Discover activities related to weather and seasons on this website.

www.sciencekids.co.nz/plants.html
Learn all about plants on this website.

Index